TEN TRAITS

of a

HEALTHY
PARENT

Dear Eric,
   To my beloved
long time friend! You
are a wonderful father
and grandfather!
      I love you,
         Ron

TEN TRAITS

of a

HEALTHY PARENT

Dr. Ron Lee Davis

Joanne Holdsworth Bouslough, Editor

Published by: Independent Publishing

Published in the United States of America

ISBN: 9781728805450

Lovingly dedicated to my grandchildren,
Caitlin, Gavin, Cami, and Griffin.

Each of you reflects the
compassion, kindness, and faith
of your mother and father.

Dr. Ron Lee Davis

Dedicated to Dads and Moms.

Parenting is your greatest joy,
and your greatest challenge.

Yours is a divine calling.

Joanne Holdsworth Bouslough

"Drawing out the dreams of our children is only one of many ways that we value the personhood of each child."

Dr. Ron Lee Davis

CONTENTS

PROLOGUE

Our daughter, Rachael was born eleven weeks prematurely. She weighed three pounds at birth, and within a few days, her weight dropped even further. Soon Rachael's breathing became labored. The physicians determined that she had contracted "Hyaline Membrane Disease," a serious respiratory distress.

Soon this infection became complicated by several additional lung infections. From the hospital where she was born, she was rushed by ambulance to Children's Hospital in downtown Minneapolis. There she was cared for in an incubator for the first six weeks of her life. Each day was a life struggle for our little Rachael, and several times we received middle of the night calls to come to the hospital immediately, as our baby might not live until morning.

Gradually, Rachael gained weight and strength. Finally, she was allowed to come home, but with the requirement that she remain in isolation for one full year. Only my wife, my mother, and I were allowed to care for her. During this difficult first year, she had several setbacks, including a severe bout with pneumonia. Scores of beloved friends from around the country prayed daily for her healing as our neonatologist told us that he had never seen or read of a baby born so prematurely, with so many lung infections, who had lived.

After one full year of isolation, God in His Grace did bring His healing touch. Today, over forty years later, Rachael is healthy and happily married with four children.

Our son Nathan was born three years after Rachael's birth. It was a second difficult pregnancy. So my heart is doubly grateful for the wonderful privilege of being a parent to two beloved children who continue to bless and encourage me. They are not only my daughter and son, they are both dear and beloved friends.

Over the past forty years, I have sought to understand from both scripture and psychological research what it would mean to be spiritually and emotionally healthy parents. I was fortunate to grow up in a Christian home with a loving and compassionate mother and father. I was also blessed with the privilege of serving as a youth pastor for many years at a wonderful church in Minneapolis where I ministered to hundreds of teenagers. Finally, I was favored by God to have many wise and caring mentors come into my life to guide me in my growing understanding of what it meant to be a Christian father.

Over twenty-five years ago, I began to teach a series called, "Traits of a Healthy Parent."

Through the years, I taught this material at various churches, conferences, men's retreats and adult education classes. Many came alongside me to further guide me to understand the implications of these emerging traits. This book is the end result of these many years of writing, teaching, and refining the material.

Next to my relationship with Christ, the greatest joy of my life has been to be a parent.

I have made many mistakes, falling short over and over again, and I am grateful for the grace and forgiveness my children have extended to me. Through the joys and heartaches of parenting, these ten traits have constantly guided me, and helped me to regain God's perspective on being a parent. May they instruct and encourage you so that you may be all that God would have you become as a healthy parent.

CHAPTER 1

A Healthy Parent will demonstrate unconditional love to his or her children, both verbally and nonverbally.

"Let the children come to me, because the kingdom of God belongs to such as these."

Jesus Christ, Mark 10:14

My longtime friend, Dr. Leighton Ford and his wife Jeanie were being interviewed many years ago on a nationally syndicated radio program. In the course of the interview, Leighton and Jeanie were asked how the healing process was progressing in the aftermath of the tragic death of their son, Sandy who had passed away in his early twenties from heart failure.

In response to this question, Leighton shared these insightful words, "We hurt deeply. There is a wound in our hearts that may turn to a scar one day, but that wound will never fully heal.

"Yet, there are some parents for whom we hurt more than ourselves. We hurt even more for those parents who never demonstrated genuine affection, compassion, and unconditional love for their child, and now, that opportunity is gone.

"We hurt deeply for those parents who were raising a child in their home, and now that child has grown into a young adult. There has been brokenness there, or maybe even estrangement, and now, that child is taken away. The parent lives not only with *grief,* but also with *guilt.* God in His grace can give freedom in time from that guilt, but often that heartache remains for a lifetime. Sadly, some parents have never taken the time to demonstrate unconditional love to their children."

My goal in this chapter is to encourage us to expand our vision in terms of a crucial trait that is foundational to all other characteristics of healthy parenting: *unconditional love*. I feel deeply fortunate to live out my life knowing that I grew up in a home where I can never remember a time when I did not feel loved. My ninety-four year old mother, who passed away a few years ago, was an extremely kind, gracious, and loving Christian. Before their deaths, my father and my brother were similarly compassionate and demonstrative in their love for me.

Yet, even in a home like mine, it was often easy for me as a child to *feel* as though I would be more loved, or more valued, or more accepted, if I could just *perform* better. Put another way, I am not sure that as a child I always *felt* unconditionally loved. Nor do I believe that any child in any family always feels unconditionally loved. All of us carry with us some brokenness in different areas of our lives, and often in our brokenness, we will fail to consistently demonstrate unconditional love to our children.

Indeed, while the term "unconditional love" has gained broad acceptance in our society, in reality, it is often not understood, nor is it practiced within our homes. The emotionally healthy parent, therefore, has a passion to be continually communicating to each of his children in all sorts of ways these words: *"There is nothing that you will ever do that will ever make me love you more, and there is nothing that you will ever do that could ever make me love you less."*

We understand as Christian parents that at best, out in the world, from time to time, our children may be loved conditionally based upon their performances in some area of academics, sports, music, or dance. But, the home is to be a *haven* where children know deeply within their hearts that without question, they are loved unconditionally and extravagantly, and that this love is *not* based upon any performance or choice that they make.

We communicate that verbally, and increasingly Christian psychologists are telling us that of equal or greater importance is the nonverbal communication of unconditional love. Dr. Ross Campbell, noted Christian child psychologist writes these words, "The most obvious way of conveying our love to a child is through physical contact. Yet studies show that most fathers touch their children only when necessity demands it. Especially, they are reluctant to touch their sons. Research shows that girl infants receive five times as much physical contact as boy infants, which is a key reason why six times as many young boys as girls are seen in psychiatric clinics around the country."

"Fathers," he writes, "remember that physical contact, especially the more affectionate type is vital to boys, especially during their younger years. The younger the boy, the more vital affectionate contact is to him, while with a girl, physical contact increases in importance as she becomes older, and reaches a zenith around the age of eleven. Nothing breaks my heart more than an eleven year old girl who is not receiving consistent, adequate emotional nourishment from her father." Indeed, we all know that many teenage girls, when they are not receiving that kind of nourishment and support from their fathers, will seek it out from other males, often with tragic consequences like pregnancy and abortion, guilt and shame.

A growing number of Christian psychologists are teaching us that there are four primary ways that we demonstrate unconditional love to a child. They are:

1. Focused attention
2. Eye contact
3. Physical contact
4. Consistent verbal reassurance

The first of these four ways, "focused attention" may be one of the most difficult responsibilities to master, especially in our present culture. Our ongoing relationships with our children demand more authentic *presence,* more consistent *intentionality,* more *courage* to turn away from the technological diversions that surround us. Simply stated, a child will not *feel* focused attention if we are peering at our phones, televisions, or computer screens while he or she is trying to share a feeling with us.

Brendon Burchard writes well when he states, "In a modern world plagued by distraction, our greatest work in becoming better lovers is in reconnecting with those who have already given us their hearts. We have to finally stop all the looking about, and once more peer into the eyes of those we adore. We have to ask them more questions: How was their day *really*? What are they struggling with? What would make them feel more alive and happy? How can we connect with and care for them better? Is there a way that we can demonstrate even more affection and appreciation for them?"

In this season of my life, I am regularly interacting with my four young grandchildren. As we share our lives together, I frequently kneel down, make eye contact with them, focus my attention on their needs with all distractions put aside, and have my hand on their shoulder or around their back. During our one-on-one weekly dates, I prayerfully seek to find the appropriate moments to share reassuring statements like,

"Caitlin, you are such a kind and loving leader. Gavin, you have such courage to take a stand for what is right. Cami, you bring joy and laughter to so many. Griffin, I'm proud of the way you share with your friends." Often, I end these conversations with the simple reassurance that I will always love them, no matter what choices they make for the rest of their lives.

The sunlight slanted over the Rockies, painting the trees, the ground, and the houses with a warm golden glow. My brother Paul and I were jogging on the running trails that wound among the hills west of Denver, near the Red Rocks Amphitheater. I remember the scene clearly, the dirt paths beaten down by the shoes of many other runners, the hilly and wooded countryside, the brush where the deer would pause and stare in amazement at these strange humans.

Paul and I ran this ten mile course every evening during our stay with his family. It was a good time to be alone with my brother. We took the course at an easy pace, and we talked as we ran. We talked about a lot of things, but mostly reminisced about the days when we were growing up in Iowa, about the good times that we had, about our mom and dad, about our faith in Christ.

"Ron," Paul said as we pounded down a gently sloping grade, "you and I are both following Christ, just like Mom and Dad used to pray that we would when we were kids. Why do you think that is?" I thought about it for a few strides. Then, I responded, "From a human perspective, I'd have to say that it's the way Mom and Dad lived. They lived what they said they believed," I continued. "The things that Dad preached in the pulpit, the things that they both taught us at home, the times that they disciplined us, it all matched up with the way that they lived. The love that they spoke of at Sunday school and church is the love that they modeled to us every day at home."

"Right," said Paul, huffing slightly as we started up a hill. "I thought that's what you'd say. Integrity. walking your talk. When kids see that in their parents, they want to live that way, too. Dad was the finest man I ever knew. He always lived what he believed. He loved us unconditionally. I want to be that kind of dad to my boys." And, Paul was that kind of dad.

A Healthy Parent will demonstrate unconditional love to his or her children both verbally and nonverbally.

CHAPTER 2

A Healthy Parent will seek to value
the personhood of each child.

"Children have very deep feelings just the way parents do, and are striving to understand those feelings and to better respond to them is the most important task in the world."

Fred Rogers,

Creator of Mr. Rogers' Neighborhood

Over the past five decades, I've been honored to be in the presence of many people who were very near the moment of their death. As we have visited together, either in a hospital room or the friend's own home, one common theme reoccurs. In our tender, vulnerable moments together, often the dying person will say to me words like, "Now at this point in my life, all that matters to me is to stay close to Christ, and to love my family." All of us yearn to love our families, and as we transition from this life into eternity, that love will sustain us and strengthen us.

As parents, we long to show love to our children, yet often, we don't specifically and concretely know how to value and esteem them. I believe that we value the personhood of a child in the following five ways.

First, by respecting our children's opinions. A friend of mine who was a pastor for many years, shared with me that on one occasion, a teenage boy came into his office, and blurted out these words, "To my dad, I am nothing but a 'comma'." The pastor was taken aback, and he asked, "What do you mean when you say that to your dad, you're 'nothing but a comma'?"

The boy responded, "Every time I come into the room, and I want to talk to my dad, he is always on the phone. He's either talking to a friend about sports, or he's setting up a golf game, or talking about a business deal. Then I come in, and want to say something to him, he stops long enough for me to speak. As soon as I'm done saying what I want to say, he picks up the conversation with his friend right where he left off. To my dad, I am nothing but a 'comma'."

We value the personhood of our children by respecting their opinions. We understand that as our children begin to grow up, and move toward the adolescent years, this becomes more difficult. But we train ourselves with active listening skills so that we can really understand the opinions of our children, even though they are often far different than those that we may hold.

Second, we value the personhood of each child by respecting each child's privacy. It was Billy Graham who wrote that never in all of his life had he entered any of the rooms of his children without first knocking. From kindergarten through grade school, junior high, and high school, "Never once, did I ever enter any of the rooms of my children without first knocking." Why? Because we value the personhood of our children by respecting their privacy.

Albert Schweitzer, whom we remember as that great physician who cared for the poorest of the poor in West Central Africa, once wrote that people of every age need an inner sanctum, a safe place where they can go to be alone, alone with their dreams, their prayers, and their tears. Scores of sociologists have suggested that one of the greatest struggles of inner city children, and I've seen this first hand, is that inner city children grow up in one big room in a tenant apartment building. There they feel like they have no solitude to develop their own senses of identity, self-worth and personhood. We honor, revere and value our children by respecting their privacy.

Third, we value our children by trusting them. Over the past four decades, we have been hearing and reading about a term called "toxic shame." John Bradshaw is generally recognized as the person who popularized this phrase. Scores of people in our society feel that they have experienced "toxic shame" from their parents when they were children, and they desperately don't want to reproduce that characteristic now as they are parenting their children.

One great way to shame your child is to constantly distrust him, to communicate in all sorts of ways that you as my child are in no way trustworthy. In time, very often a child becomes exactly the very thing that he is told that he is by his parent. As anyone who has worked extensively with teenagers would know, frequently in the adolescent years, the teenager may begin to feel,

"Well, if that's what my parents think I am, then that's what I will be." *Expectation tends to foretell performance.* That's a statement that every healthy parent ought to commit to memory!

A classic example would be the many studies that have been researched within the discipline of educational psychology often referred to as "Student Performance Based upon Teacher Expectation Studies." If we were to summarize all of the scores of studies in educational psychology that have been researched into one scenario, the scenario would go like this: "Miss Smith is a third grade teacher. She is told ahead of time that in the new school year, she will have twenty students. She is told that ten of these third graders are outstanding students who will be very compliant. She is given the names of the ten students.

"She is also told that she will have ten students who are academically challenged, and unruly. Again, she is given a list of names.

Sure enough, at the end of the semester, the vast majority of the "outstanding" students have the highest grades, and the slower learners have the worst. In reality, the names were given to Miss Smith *at random.* "

Expectation tends to foretell performance. It is a verifiable psychological reality, and more importantly, this truth is affirmed in scripture itself.

We have powerful evidence in all of the disciplines that children tend to become what we communicate to them. Parents do far more good when we have wonderful expectations for our children, for how great that they are going to be for God, then to give them the message that we are looking for ways to distrust them, to raise suspicion about them, and to shame them.

Fourth, we value the personhood of each child by taking the time to get to know the child by the longhand of personhood. Years ago, psychologist David Elkind wrote a classic book entitled <u>The Hurried Child</u>. In the book he writes, "When we parents are under stress, we need shortcuts. We need to get things done quickly. So, we don't take the time to deal carefully and in depth with our children. Parents under stress tend to see their children in the shorthand of symbols rather than the often hard to decipher 'longhand' of personhood."

Examples of the "shorthand of symbols" include statements like:

My son is an athlete.
Your daughter is an "A" student.
This boy is a computer whiz.

However, "My son has a sensitive, melancholy temperament. He is very tender toward the less popular students in his class. He can be prone to mild depression, and can appear to become anxious when feeling overwhelmed." That's the "longhand" of personhood.

Presbyterian pastor Fred Rogers, better known simply as "Mr. Rogers" from his popular children's television program, writes well when he states, "Children have very deep feelings just the way parents do, just the way everybody does, and are striving to understand those feelings and to better respond to them is what I feel is the most important task in our world." As we strive to understand our children's deepest feelings, we will be modeling our commitment to know our children in the longhand of personhood.

Fifth, we value the personhood of each child by believing in his or her dreams. When a child takes the risk of sharing a dream, vision, or meaningful idea with mom or dad, the most damaging thing that a parent can do to a child is to respond with:

"You've got to be kidding"!
"You're not serious, are you?"
"I can't believe that you said that"!

One of my favorite scriptural paraphrases for parents is found in Proverbs 20:5: *"A dream in the heart of a child is like deep water, but the parent of understanding draws it out."* A dream in the heart of your daughter is like deep water, the Bible says, and the understanding parent is going to take the time to draw it out. And, the same is true for your boy. This is a major task for every parent. Parenthetically, it often means that our understanding includes recognizing that their dreams may be far different than our dreams for them.

You have a child who has a desire to build things, and you have never been interested in construction. Now you begin to take an interest. You never make light of that dream; you always affirm it, because you want to encourage his dream.

Do you have a child who is interested in history? You've never been drawn to this subject, but now you begin to take an interest in all kinds of historical facts. Again, you never make light of this dream, and think, "Well, he's good at that, he doesn't need affirmation from me." Rather, we understand that we are called to draw out our children's dreams.

Through my brother Paul, I developed a friendship with a man who was 6'10", and was an outstanding college basketball player. Along with my brother, he developed the "Shot Doctor" basketball camps that were held at various sites all around the United States. This friend of mine, a great Christian father, had a son. At the age of 14 years, and in 8th grade, his son was 6'5". Do you know what the 6'5" son loved to do more than anything else? He loved to dance! He wanted to take dance lessons, and to be in dance shows. My friend told me that his response to his son was, "I'm doing everything that I can to get you into every dance class you want to attend." He then said to me, "Ron, I thought that he'd want to play basketball, but, I think maybe that was my dream. I want to draw out *his* dream because the scripture says, 'the dream in the heart of a child is like deep water, but a parent of understanding is always going to be drawing it out.'"

Drawing out the dreams of our children is only one of many ways that we value their personhood. A Healthy Parent will value the personhood of each child.

"A dream in the heart of a child is like deep water, but the parent of understanding draws it out."

Proverbs 20:5 (paraphrase)

CHAPTER 3

A Healthy Parent will take the time to get to know his or her child according to his or her own uniqueness.

"One of the foremost responsibilities of Christian parents is to enjoy their children.

Gordon Cosby

"Cat's in the Cradle"

My child arrived just the other day.
He came to the world in the usual way.
But, there were planes to catch, and bills to pay.
He learned to walk while I was away.
And, he was talkin' 'fore I knew it, and as he grew
He'd say, "I'm gonna' be like you, Dad,
You know I'm gonna' be like you."

And, the Cat's in the Cradle and the Silver Spoon,
Little Boy Blue, and the Man in the Moon.
"When you comin' home, Dad?"
"I don't know when, but we'll get together then, Son.
You know we'll have a good time then."

My son turned ten just the other day.
He said, "Thanks for the ball, Dad, come on, let's play.
Can you teach me to throw?" I said, "Not today,
I got a lot to do." He said, "That's okay."
And, he walked away, but his smile never dimmed,
And, said, "I'm gonna' be like him, yeah,
You know I'm gonna' be like him."

And, the Cat's in the Cradle and the Silver Spoon,
Little Boy Blue, and the Man in the Moon.
"When you comin' home, Dad?"
"I don't know when, but we'll get together then, Son.
You know we'll have a good time then."

Well, he came home from college just the other day
So much like a man I just had to say,
"Son, I'm proud of you; can you sit for a while?"
He shook his head, and said with a smile
"What I'd really like, Dad, is to borrow the car keys.
See you later. Can I have them, please?"

And, the Cat's in the Cradle and the Silver Spoon,
Little Boy Blue and the Man in the Moon.
"When you comin' home, Son?"
"I don't know when, but we'll get together then, Dad.
You know we'll have a good time then.

I've long since retired; my son's moved away.
I called him up just the other day.
I said, "I'd like to see you, if you don't mind."
He said, "I'd love to, Dad, if I can find the time.
You see, my new job's a hassle,
And the kids have the flu.
But, it's sure nice talking to you, Dad.
It's sure nice talking to you."

And, as I hung up the phone, it occurred to me
He'd grown up just like me.
My boy was just like me.

And, the Cat's in the Cradle and the Silver Spoon
Little Boy Blue and the Man in the Moon.
"When you comin' home, Son?"
"I don't know when, but we'll get together then, Dad.
You know we'll have a good time then."

That number one best-selling song, familiar to many, was written by Harry Chapin. Harry Chapin is dead today. Years ago, he was tragically killed in an automobile accident. He has no more time to get to know his boy. But, before he died, he wrote this prophetic song for those of us parents who do.

The little boy with both rage and tears in his eyes came up to his father who was an active Christian layman getting ready to attend yet another committee meeting down at church. He looked up at his dad, and said, "Dad, I hate Jesus!" The father was taken aback, and he asked,

"What do you mean, you hate Jesus? I thought you loved Jesus." And, the little boy responded, "Well, you know, Dad, I've decided that I hate Jesus because all Jesus ever does is take you away from me."

My thesis for this chapter is simply this: One of the greatest contributions that you can make to your child's life is to know him, to really *know* him. In fact, I believe that next to leading your child to Christ, the single greatest contribution that you can make in the life of your child is to know him or her because you cannot deeply love a child whom you do not know. And, further, you cannot properly *raise* a child whom you do not know as we will see in our text from scripture.

In Proverbs 22:6, we read these familiar words: "Train up a child in the way he should go, and when he is old, he will not depart from it." Now, through the years, the standard interpretation of this verse has often gone something like this: "Be certain that your children are in Sunday School from early on in life, and teach them the Ten Commandments and some prayers that they can say at meal time and bedtime. As your child grows up, even though he may go through a time of rebellion in adolescence or young adulthood, when he is older, he will eventually come back to the faith.

Growing up in the church, I've heard a dozen or more sermons interpreting Proverbs 22:6 in essentially this way. However, a growing number of serious Bible students have come to suggest that far more is taught here than the ingredients I just mentioned, as important as they may be.

Literally, the verse could be translated from the Hebrew, "Train up a child *according to his own way,* and when he is old, he will not depart from the faith." The Hebrew word here is "dereck." It means that as we train our children, they should be trained according to their own uniqueness. I would paraphrase Proverbs 22:6 as follows: Modify the training for each of your children based upon their distinctive, God-given temperaments and unique characteristics, and then, when each child matures, he will not retreat from the guidance you have given him.

It was Ray Stedman, the wonderful pastor at the Peninsula Bible Church in Palo Alto, author of scores of Bible commentaries, and the greatest spiritual father to me next to my own dad who showed me a deeper understanding of the Hebrew text here in Proverbs. Thankfully, he shared the insight with me before my children were born. A child who is properly trained is one who is trained in keeping with his or her uniqueness, in his or her own way, not in our preconceived way.

I was a youth pastor for ten years. Parents used to come into my office, and they would say, "We don't understand, Ron. One of our children is very rebellious. Our other child is very compliant, and we've trained them exactly the same!" Then we would get into a conversation where I'd suggest that maybe it wasn't always wise to train them in the same way because your children aren't exactly the same. A form of discipline or praise that might be effective with one of your children won't work well at all with another.

Highly regarded Bible teacher Charles Ryrie puts it this way in one of his Bible commentaries: "The phrase in Proverbs 22:6 'in the way he should go' must take into account the child's individuality and inclinations, and be in keeping with his degree of physical and mental development; in other words, *with his uniqueness.*"

They are unique, you know. Take birth order. Twenty-one of the first twenty-three astronauts in this country were "first born." We can take virtually any pioneer leadership position in American culture, and we will find a similar ratio. First born tend to be serious, high achievers; lastborn tend to be light-hearted, fun lovers. Yours may be just the reverse, but one study over a fifteen year period with over one thousand children observed concluded, "First born will tend to be more adult-oriented, leaders, responsible, mature for their age, ambitious, and assertive. Last born will tend to be easy going, cheerful, stubborn, light-hearted, unconcerned, gentle."

Dr. Kevin Leman, a Christian psychologist who has devoted much of his life to a study of birth order writes in his helpful book, <u>The Birth Order Book,</u> "The first born attempts to conquer the world. The last born lives in harmony with the world." He goes on to suggest, "First born tend to be perfectionists, reliable, conscientious, well-organized, serious and scholarly. Middle born tend to be mediators, avoiding of conflict, independent, loyal. Last born tend to be charming, people-persons, precocious, engaging." My brother Paul and I were textbook first born and last born.

Now, I fully realize that these patterns don't always hold true, and it becomes more complicated when you are parents of four, five or more children, or when children are more than three or four years apart. But, we do know that these patterns hold true in 80% of all adults in American culture.

Gretchen Rubin, in her excellent book <u>Better than Before</u>, describes four styles that children have in relationship to expectations placed upon them by parents and teachers. The four styles are:

1. **Upholders** Upholders respond readily to outer and inner expectations placed upon them.

2. **Questioners** This style questions expectations placed upon them, and will meet the expectations only if they think it makes sense to do so.

3. **Obligers** Obligers will meet outer expectations, but struggle to meet expectations that they place upon themselves.

4. **Rebels** This type will consistently resist all expectations placed upon them, by others, by themselves.

Rubin suggests that research teaches us that most personalities are either Questioners or

Obligers. Our challenge as parents is to make certain that we *know* our children so deeply that we understand their primary tendencies in relationship to expectations.

Add to birth order and expectation styles factors like temperament: Is my child sanguine (social, enthusiastic), or melancholic (wise, soft spoken)? Is my child choleric (strong willed, task oriented), or phlegmatic (serene, relaxed)? Then, add factors like personality types. Is my child more analytical, or more sensory? Is my child more "Type A," driven, or more "Type B," amiable? Now we begin to recognize that it is going to take lots and lots of time to get to know each child, according to his or her own uniqueness.

If this is indeed what Proverbs 22:6 means, then the Bible should verify it in other scriptures. Martin Luther taught us that the very first principle of biblical interpretation is that scripture *verifies* other scripture, scripture *validates* other scripture, scripture *affirms* other scripture, and no one part of scripture ought to ever be interpreted in such a way as to render it in conflict with the whole of scripture.

As we look at scripture, we find virtually without exception, two children born into the same family are entirely different and unique. Centuries before psychologists ever started thinking about birth order, Jesus taught us about it. "The Prodigal Son" is a textbook example of a responsible first born working hard in the fields all day, while the last born wants to go off and enjoy his life in rebellion, squandering the family inheritance. Were they alike? Not at all.

What about our children? Are they alike? Probably not. Or, have we ever taken enough time to *really* get to know them according to their own uniqueness so that if the opportunity presented itself, each of us could articulate the differences, the nuances in temperament between each of our family members?

Train up a child according to his own uniqueness. The testimony of scores of young people who entered the door of my office when I was in youth ministry often went something like this. "Ron, I'm so different than my older brother, but Mom and Dad want me to be just like him!" I've observed that so often the seedbed for adolescent rebellion in its many forms is rooted in the parents' failure to get to know and accept each child as being unique.

As we are getting to know our children, and to respect their uniqueness, I offer a very important guideline that can better enable that process to take place:

Take delight in your children. This is a message that we sometimes fail to emphasize.

There are lots of sermons focusing on effective discipline, and other aspects of parenting, but for those of us who grew up in the church, how often have we heard that we have an absolute responsibility before God to take delight in our children?

Sam Keen tells of the last visit that he had with his father. His dad was on his death bed. Sam knelt down beside the bed, and these were the last words that he said to him before his dad died. "Dad, you have always been there whenever any of us children needed you. And across the years, you have given us one of the greatest gifts that any parent could give: you took delight in us. In all sorts of ways, you let us know that you were glad that we were here, that we had value in your eyes, that our presence was a joy, and not a burden to you. Dad, you took *delight* in us." And then, Sam Keen's father quietly passed. How are we doing these days at taking delight in our children?

Before his death, prolific author and pastor Gordon Cosby argued convincingly from scripture that one of the foremost responsibilities of all parents is to enjoy their children. How are we doing at fulfilling that biblical admonition?

We need to create all sorts of enjoyable activities for our children on a regular basis. Our family was fortunate that from the time that our children were very young, we were able to have weekly fun-filled family nights. When our children became adults, one statement that they would make to us regularly is, "You know, it was so great to grow up in a Christian home because there was so much fun there"!

I love the words of Irish playwright George Bernard Shaw: "We don't stop playing because we grow old; we grow old because we stop playing." From the time my children were babies, we played together. In addition to weekly family nights, I developed the tradition of weekly one-on-one breakfasts with each of our children.

Susanna Wesley, often considered the founder of Methodism, and mother of Christian leaders John and Charles Wesley, bore nineteen children. Several were lost as infants, but for those who lived, Susanna gave an hour a week for a special "date" with each child. When the children had grown into adulthood, and left home, she devoted that same hour during the week to pray for each individual child.

Today, I continue weekly one-on-one dates with my four young grandchildren who live nearby. Whether we are playing air hockey, bowling, playing tag on the beach, seeing a fun family movie in a local theater, painting ceramics, or jogging with our family dog, I always seek to convey that I take genuine, authentic *delight* in my children and grandchildren.

How about us dads and moms? Are we creating an atmosphere of joy for our children as we take the time to get to know them according to their own uniqueness? Train up a child according to his own uniqueness, and when he is old, he will not depart from the training that he has received. A Healthy Parent will take the time to get to know the child according to his or her own uniqueness.

"We don't stop playing because we grow old, we grow old because we stop playing."

George Bernhard Shaw

CHAPTER 4

A healthy parent will seek to discern unhealthy intergenerational patterns, and break the cycle of those patterns.

"God has given each of us a role to play in the building of great cathedrals: boys and girls who will become spiritually and emotionally healthy men and women of God."

Dr. Ron Lee Davis

In the film "Parenthood," we encounter a kind, anxious, compulsive father named Gil Buckman, wonderfully portrayed by Steve Martin. At one pivotal moment in the film, Gil asks his wife in exasperation, "Where does our son get his obsessive behavior? Why is our boy so compulsive?" And then, after a knowing glance from his wife, their eyes meet, and he knows the answer. "Our son is so obsessive because *I* am so obsessive. Our boy is so compulsive because *I* am so compulsive." And then, with deep sincerity, and no small degree of heartache, Gil says softly, "You know, when your kid is born, you feel he seems so perfect. You haven't made any mistakes yet. But then, the baby grows up, and he becomes just like me."

We must admit that there is so often this powerful linkage between parent and child when it comes to our brokenness and character flaws. All of us who are parents want to pass onto our children only what is good in us, and none of what is defective. But, if we are candid, we know that at times, the very character flaws that we see in ourselves begin to emerge in our children.

This phenomenon ought not to surprise us because we see examples of this reality throughout scripture. The impatient nature of the parent is often passed onto the child. The demeaning, shaming, profane tongue of the parent is often passed onto the child. The parent's procrastinating temperament is frequently observed in the child. The manipulative technique utilized by the parent often becomes part of a child's emotional response as well.

Frequently, friends have painfully expressed confessions to me similar to these words: "You know, Ron, the character flaw that I most disliked in my dad, I now see not only emerging in my own life, but sadly is becoming apparent in the life of my child."

In Exodus 34:7, we read: "The sins of the parents shall be visited upon the children and upon the grandchildren, and onto the third and fourth generation." This verse is stated explicitly twice in the Old Testament. Its truth is affirmed implicitly throughout all of scripture.

The word "visited" in the Hebrew text carries with it the idea of God continuing to allow those character flaws in our lives to continue on in our children's lives, *if they go unchecked.*

Accordingly, every time that we discover a character flaw in our lives, the key question becomes "Will I now do everything that I can in partnership with God to stop, to halt, to put to an end this intergenerational character flaw?"

Family systems psychologists have given to us helpful insights in relationship to the Exodus 34:7

passage. They suggest that research indicates that very often, a young married couple carries with them unresolved conflicts toward one or more of their parents. If these conflicts continue to remain unsettled, the couple can begin to grow apart within their marriage. In reality, as this relational distance grows between them, they become emotionally divorced. They begin to live as married singles.

The couple then abandons directing any attention or love toward each other, and when a child enters this broken system, he or she becomes the recipient of all of their feelings. When a family is formed, it's members are very connected emotionally. They become interdependent as they connect and react to each other. A change in how one person functions will cause changes in the people around him or her.

Even at a young age, and without words, a child senses that something is very wrong. Because of the dynamics of this family system, the child can often become confused and emotionally distraught. Frequently, the child is viewed as the person who is having problems, when in reality, he is only one part of a dysfunctional family, passed on from one generation to another. The words of scripture ring true: "The sins of the parents shall be visited upon the children and the grandchildren, unto the third and fourth generation."

The truth of this strategic verse for parents is affirmed throughout scripture, most notably in the tragic family system we discover when we reflect on the life of Abraham. A careful study into the character of Abraham reveals a tragic flaw: when Abraham was under duress, he became deceptive. If we research the life of Abraham's son Isaac, we observe the same exact character flaw. When Isaac was under duress, he became deceptive. Isaac's son Jacob did not escape this character flaw, nor did eleven of Jacob's twelve sons. Four generations of deception: Abraham, Isaac, Jacob, and eleven of the twelve sons of Jacob.

At some point, an emotionally healthy parent must rise up and say in his or her own heart, "Enough is enough! I am going to become consciously aware of the intergenerational character flaws in our family. And, I am going to do all that I can in partnership with our loving God to break the cycle. I'll begin first in my own life, and then as I see the character flaw emerging in my son or my daughter."

How can the cycle be broken? I offer three crucial answers.

First, we will begin to break intergenerational character flaws when we are experiencing a vital daily walk with Christ. Just before I left home to begin my seminary studies, my father gently said to me one fall evening, "Ron, the most important decision you will make through the years of your seminary training is to be certain you maintain a warm, daily walk with Jesus Christ." Wise counsel.

We begin our journey toward the breaking of intergenerational character flaws by maintaining a winsome, loving daily walk with Christ, and *by leading our children into a meaningful relationship with God.* Chapter 9 of this book is devoted to understanding this pivotal process.

Suffice it to say here that we need all of the help that we can receive to break the character flaws in our own lives. We need all of the help that we can receive to be involved in the process of breaking those flaws in our children's and grandchildren's lives. There is nothing in all of life that is going to help us and our family members break intergenerational character flaws more than to have a personal, exuberant, loving, daily walk with God.

Second, we need to consistently ask God to give us wisdom and discernment as we study and observe our children and their potential character flaws. James 1:5 guides us to understand that if we are lacking in wisdom, we need to ask God, and He will grant it to us liberally.

To study our children takes time. Accordingly, the sensitive Christian parent is continually asking himself the question, "What can I do to simplify my life so that I can spend more time with my children, so that I may be able to study them, and affirm the wonderful character qualities that I see emerging in them, as well as acknowledge the character flaws that I recognize are developing.

After significant research, one psychologist writes these words: "What the very young want, and urgently need first is not education or socialization, but rather the affection and unhurried attention of their parents." When my children were growing up, I would read with them at bedtime every night. We especially enjoyed reading through <u>The Lion, the Witch, and the Wardrobe</u> series by C.S. Lewis.

When my children were growing up, after our reading times, and just before evening prayers, we would visit about our day just past. As my children were generally in no hurry to have to go to sleep, this was an ideal time to just come to know each other more deeply. Through the countless hours of these bedtime chats, I observed a great deal about the character, the personality, the joys and the fears of Rachael and Nathan. I'm thankful today that we took the time together for those moments of loving and sharing.

Third, as parents we need to understand that generally, an unchecked character flaw will escalate, not subside. Both scripture and psychological research affirm this hard truth. Because of this challenging reality, every Christian parent must seek to build this important truth into his or her heart: *Passivity is an enemy.* Often in my ten year tenure as a youth pastor of a large Midwestern church, I encountered a child or an adolescent with an accelerating character flaw, and the response of the parent would be one of passivity. Passivity for a Christian parent is always an enemy because we understand that an unchecked character flaw emerging in one of our children will not remain in neutral; it will generally accelerate.

One of the stories that guides me greatly these days as a parent and grandparent is one about a simple man who centuries ago, went to three stone masons, and asked them what they were doing. The first stone mason said, "Oh, I'm laying bricks." The second stone mason answered, "Oh, I'm putting up a wall." But the third stone mason replied, "What am I doing? I'm building a great cathedral."

My prayer is that we as parents don't see our roles as just laying bricks, buying groceries, paying bills, fixing dinner. But, rather that we believe with a grateful heart that God has given each of us a role to play in the building of great cathedrals: boys and girls who will become spiritually and emotionally healthy men and women for God. And, as we capture this vision, we will begin in partnership with our living Lord to break the cycle so that no longer will the "sins of the parents be visited upon the children, the grandchildren, and onto the third and fourth generations." A Healthy Parent will seek to discern unhealthy intergenerational patterns, and to break the cycle of those patterns.

"In a modern world plagued by distraction, our greatest work is in reconnecting with those who have already given us their hearts."

Brendon Burchard

CHAPTER 5

A Healthy Parent models a commitment that when problems arise, they are openly confronted and talked through using positive communication skills.

"The purpose of loving confrontation is to heal, not to cripple. It is to help, not to hurt. It is to restore, not to shame."

Dr. Ron Lee Davis

Some time ago in the state of Illinois, a Christian gentleman was honored as being "The Outstanding State Trooper of the Year." The governor of the state of Illinois made this comment: "I want you all to recognize that not once in this man's entire career has there ever been one piece of paper put in his personnel file containing a complaint that was negative or critical of him. Not once in twenty years has there ever been an accusation made against him by any of the individuals whom he arrested."

The governor went on to say, "Not once has there ever been any kind of questionable conduct that has been brought forth regarding this state trooper. This man has never verbally abused or mistreated anyone whom he had had to arrest. This record is literally unheard of in the state of Illinois."

After the banquet, a journalist came up to this state trooper and asked him what the keys to his success were. The trooper, a rather shy and reserved man, was reluctant to comment, but finally responded by saying, "Well, there have been two keys that have helped my success over the last twenty years. The first key has been that whenever I've had to stop a car, I get out of my vehicle, and as I'm walking toward the car, I always softly recite to myself Proverbs 15:1: 'A soft answer turns away wrath, a soft answer turns away wrath.' When I get to that car, and I lean over to talk with the individuals, I always respond to them in a tone of voice that is softer than the one that they are using with me."

"My second guideline has been that whenever I'm called to apprehend or subdue someone who's been drinking too much, I get out of my car, and as I am walking toward that person, I say to myself, 'This person is not a drunk. This person is somebody's husband who has been drinking too much. This person is not a drunk. This person is someone's daughter who has been drinking too much.'"

When problems arise with our children, we parents would do well to remember scriptures like, "A soft answer turns away wrath," and to recall that we are always going to value the person regardless of the conduct that that person demonstrates.

We have author John Powell to thank for putting five levels of communication into simple terms that can guide us as fathers and mothers as we seek to show our love for one another more deeply. He writes, "There are five levels of communication, and very few of us ever reach level five with our loved ones."

Level One: Cliches "How's it going?" "What's up?" "Have a good day"! Every culture has clichés, and it is very seldom that they have significant meaning attached to them.

Level Two: Facts and Reports Examples: "I saw the film 'Coco' with my grandson, Griffin." Or, "The Vikings play the Bears Sunday."

Level Three: Opinions and Convictions For example, reactions and beliefs, "I liked the film 'Coco.' It touched my heart." "When Rachael and I had dinner together, the food was delicious, but the service was poor." Powell argues convincingly from research that most families rarely move beyond levels one, two, and three in their communication with one another for any significant amount of time.

Level Four: Feelings These are expressions of emotions where the masks are taken off, and vulnerable truths are articulated. Often, tears may even be shed. At this level, a college age daughter may share, "It's so good to be home for Christmas, Mom, but I'm feeling anxious about going back to school in January. The pressure academically, socially, and morally is so great. I'm afraid." Last week, when I spent time with my daughter's family, I had a chance to genuinely share with my granddaughter, Caitlin: "I've loved the times that we've had together this week. I've so enjoyed our talks, and I'll miss you when we each go to our own homes."

Level Five: Maximum Truth Shared with Maximum Love Powell argues that this is the finest form of communication for the Christian. Unfortunately, this is too often the rarest form of communication for the Christian. It takes a deep level of spiritual and emotional maturity to traffic in Level Five; it is here that we see the expression of genuine confession of sin, authentic forgiveness, heartfelt healing, and unconditional love.

In Level Five, we share our deepest dreams. We share our most painful tears. At its root, this fifth level of communication is the heart of the Christian life in action. Its basis is Ephesians 4:15, where we are told that we are to grow up in every way unto Him who is our Head, unto Christ as we learn to speak the truth in love. This biblical truth is what gives a purpose to our Level Five sharing of feelings. Here, we don't just share random feelings. There is a purpose behind our vulnerable sharing: it is to build up one another in Christ.

While recently visiting an animal sanctuary with my 9 year old granddaughter Cami, I watched her petting a cow, and I said, "I've seen the quality of compassion in your life. Today, I'm reminded of your kindness as I see you gently care for these animals. God's going to give you a great ministry of compassion, Cami."

As we build excellent communication skills, and learn to share at the deepest levels with our loved ones, at times we are aware that these skills must be applied to confronting wrong attitudes and actions.

When loving confrontation is required with our children, especially as they move toward adolescence I offer these five guidelines which I have utilized many times in the raising of my two children, and as I relate to my four grandchildren every week.

1. **Be gentle, but firm**. Galatians 6: 1-2, when applied to parenting says this: "When you lovingly confront your child, do so in a spirit of gentleness, seeking to restore him." The Greek word for "restore" literally means, "to mend the brokenness." Whenever there is a confrontation with a child, a mature Christian parent enters that confrontation saying to himself, "I'm only seeking to mend the brokenness. I want to restore my child, and I understand that that means that I want to mend the wounds in his life."

2. **Be certain that you fully understand the situation**. Studies show that we fathers are particularly poor in this area. So, as I go into a confrontation with my child, I'm asking myself, "Do I know the whole story?" Maybe I've heard part of the story from his sister, but before any kind of

discipline or confrontation takes place, I want to be certain that I know the whole story from my child." This principle is so important that Stephen Covey in his classic book, <u>The 7 Habits of Highly Effective People,</u> lists this as the fifth habit: *"First, seek to understand, then be understood."* He stated that of the seven habits, this habit is the most difficult to apply to the family, and the single most important habit in human relationships.

3. **Verbally affirm your love for your child regularly, and throughout the conversation**. Affirm that you love your son or your daughter so that when the confrontation is over, one question that we can ask ourselves, "Did my child feel valued as a person during the confrontation?" For example, when my children were young, I trained myself so that every time that I walked out of Rachael's room and there had been a confrontation, I asked myself, "Do I think that Rachael felt valued as a person during the confrontation?" One way that we validate our children is that we constantly reassure them of our love during the conflict.

4. **Be specific**. Far better to say softly, "You know, Son, I feel that you were deceptive with me when you didn't tell me the whole story of all of the places that you were going last night," than to say, loudly, "You know what? You're nothing but a liar! You'll never be anything but a liar"! *We*

critique the behavior, we never shame the person. We don't call our children names; we never verbally abuse them.

5. **Always remember to look past the irritation to the need**. A wise parent is always looking deeper than just the irritating conduct or behavior of the child because he wants to get to the root need. Is it that my child is insecure? Does he yearn for attention? Is she crying out for help, and doesn't know any other way to get it than through inappropriate behavior? The healthy Christian parent is always seeking to reach past the irritation to the real need where restoration, healing, and hope are found.

Two final principles as we apply this fifth trait to our lives as parents:

First, be deeply concerned about the development of the character of your child. A.B. Bruce who was one of the great men of God of the nineteenth century once wrote: "None are more formidable instruments of temptation than well-meaning friends who care more about your comfort than about your character. My paraphrase of this would read: "There are few choices that a parent can make that are more tragic than to care more about your child's comfort than the development of his or her character."

Second, the purpose of loving confrontation is to heal, not to cripple. It is to help, not to hurt. It is to restore, not to shame. It is to always have a demeanor with our children that shows them "I'm not on your back, I'm on your side."

I've said to my children scores of times through the years, "No one is for you more than I am. I want you to be all that you're meant to be in Christ." When we come in that spirit, we're coming to restore the brokenness in the lives of our children. A Healthy Parent models a commitment that when problems arise, they are openly confronted and talked through using positive communication skills.

"First seek to understand, then to be understood."

Stephen R. Covey

CHAPTER 6

A Healthy Parent will understand from the time his or her children are very young that there are four major struggles that every child will face in adolescence.

"I have learned to hold onto everyone loosely."

Corrie Ten Boom

Years ago, Christian author Edith Schaeffer wrote that her role as a parent was to be "a curator in a museum of memories." My parents understood this crucial component of creating a loving family. Some of the fondest memories that my brother and I shared from our childhood were created from family vacations. Particularly, we enjoyed our annual trips to Estes Park, Colorado. Mom and Dad loved not only the picturesque mountains, streams, forests, and wildlife in the area, but also were inspired by the Fellowship of Christian Athletes conferences held in Estes Park each year.

Paul and I loved to rise early each morning, and climb various mountains in the area. As we grew older, and moved toward our teenage years, we became more adventurous in planning to climb diverse mountains. The treacherous terrain of some of our planned hikes created tension with our parents who were reluctant to allow us to climb toward certain peaks. Later in my life, I would come to understand more fully that family struggles like our differences over the risks of mountain climbing are symptomatic of the transition in childhood that we have come to call "adolescence."

As parents, we need to be aware that every child has a lot of rugged mountains to climb, particularly in adolescence. "Adolescence": the dictionary defines the term as "That time between puberty and maturity." Others have defined it differently. One psychologist defines it this way, "A time of irrational defiance." Some of us understand that definition well because we have dealt with the irrational defiance of our teenagers. We know the pain that it brings to our hearts as parents.

Whatever definition we choose, we know that the adolescent years are times of dynamic transition. Yet, as we gain an overview of the message of grace that is found within scripture, we gain this key insight: during the adolescent years, parents must seek to be as flexible as possible, adopting an attitude that is willing to learn as well as teach.

Put another way: rigidity by parents during the adolescent years will be self-defeating. The "because I said so" response has got to be replaced with all kinds of open dialogue with our children.

As parents, we are passionate about helping children work through the struggles of adolescence, and come out healthy and whole on the other side. One way that we parents help that process is to be committed to open dialogue and communication. We are working in partnership with God and with our teenagers, not just surviving, but thriving through the adolescent years. In this regard, many psychologists would assert that there are four essential struggles that every teenager will face.

The 1st Struggle for adolescents is identity. The young person between the ages of 12 and 20 begins to wrestle in a significant way with this question, "Who am I *really?* I know what Mom and Dad believe and think. When I was a child, I tended to believe and think the way that they did. Now I'm beginning to struggle with finding an authentic place for me to stand." A *healthy* teenager wrestles with issues of identity. While doing so, the adolescent will realize that in some arenas of his life, he probably is different from mom and dad. Healthy parents need to accept this struggle as part of adolescence.

The 2nd Struggle for adolescents is responsibility. In his heart, the teenager begins to feel, "You know, I'm enjoying the new freedom that Mom and Dad are giving me, and the privileges that come with it. But, I'm discovering that with this new found freedom, there's growing responsibility. I'm making significant decisions on my own. Some of these decisions are going to affect me for years to come. Some may affect me for the rest of my life! I'm starting to feel afraid and anxious about that reality. I welcome the freedom, but at times, I really want to step back from the increasing responsibility that Mom and Dad are placing upon me." The healthy parent accepts this endeavor, knowing that adolescents will struggle with responsibility.

The 3rd Struggle for adolescents is authority. Simply stated, the teenager asks himself, "Why do I always have to obey my parents?" For example, the *healthy* adolescent now begins to ask, "How often am I going to challenge Mom and Dad when they make a decision that relates to me that I don't support or that I feel is unfair?" A *healthy* adolescent will wrestle with the issue of authority.

The 4th Struggle for adolescents is conformity. We have felt it, and our teenagers will feel it: peer pressure! Sociologists and psychologists tell us that peer pressure is greater in our culture than it has been at any time in American history. The *healthy* teenager begins to wrestle in his heart with statements like these:

You know, when I was a child, I went with my parents for three hours every Sunday morning for worship and Sunday school, and I accepted that commitment.

When I was growing up, Dad & Mom put a premium on education, so I obediently did my homework every night, and I accepted that expectation.

But, now, as an adolescent, those issues and a myriad more are all up for grabs. The teenager has got to make a choice every day regarding the question: "What road am I going to take: the path of my parents, or the path of my peers?" The *healthy* adolescent struggles with conformity.

Parenthetically, another mark of adolescence is almost always apathy. The teenager is very often apathetic, complacent, and indifferent, but the wise parent understands that those characteristics are a veneer. They are a façade for the deeper issues of the teenager's insecurity in processing the four struggles.

The adolescent is beginning to realize that he's going to be making decisions that are going to have long-lasting impact on his life. But, he doesn't know how to articulate that to his parents, so he tends to cover all of that insecurity with an "I don't care" attitude. Instead of asking, "Why do you have to be so apathetic?" wise parents try to go beneath the layers of indifference, and get at the heart of the child to understand why he or she is so insecure.

Three principles can guide us as parents of teenagers.

1. Especially in the adolescent years, the wise parent will guard against rejecting his

or her child as a person of value. At times, a parent of an adolescent child will be tempted to violate the personhood of his or her teenager in the same way that he or she has just been violated by the child's demeaning response. However, with our loving God's help, we can remind ourselves of the need to understand the ongoing adolescent process.

Particularly in the adolescent years, a teenager needs *affirmation,* not *rejection.* An adolescent needs specific affirmations like, "I see more potential in you as a leader than I did a year ago." Or, "As we are giving you more freedom, I sense that you are making wiser, more mature decisions." Or, "In your life, I notice a growing concern for others, and a deeper compassion for your friends who are struggling. I'm so grateful." There are times when we as parents must reject the *behavior* of the adolescent, but during the teenage years, it is so dangerous to reject the child as a *person.*

2. **During adolescence, the wise parent will give special attention to further developing excellent communication skills, including active listening.** The sociologist, Dr. Nicholas Stinnett devoted much of his adult life to studying three thousand families. These family units were from different ethnic groups and various countries including the United States,

Germany, Austria, and Brazil. Dr. Stinnett and his colleagues studied these families carefully for several decades, and concluded that there were six essential traits that marked strong, vital families.

- **Strong families are deeply committed to one another within the family unit.** As Christians, we would say that strong families openly express their love for one another.

- **Strong families spend time together.** For example, many families schedule a weekly family night allowing each family member to take a turn selecting the activity. This was a long-standing commitment in our family as our children moved through grade school, junior high, and all of their adolescent years.

- **Strong families learn to intentionally express appreciation for one another**. As I previously mentioned, *specific* affirmations are particularly helpful in the adolescent years.

- **Strong families share a deep spiritual commitment.** As Christians, we would affirm that strong families share a deep love for Jesus Christ.

- **Strong families have the skills to solve problems together when difficulties arise.** So when a crisis occurs, big or small, each family member knows in his or her heart that this challenge will not cause the family to dissolve. Rather, each family member is confident that *together* the family will resolve difficulties.

- Strong families have developed excellent communication skills. For years, I kept these six traits on my desk to read daily. All six are so important, but during the adolescent years, number six is especially important. Parents must set the pace in their families to model excellent communication skills.

3. **The personal convictions which an adolescent decides upon will stand the test of time far better than convictions forced upon him by his parents.** Studies indicate that adolescents raised in ultra-rigid homes tend to overtly rebel as they move through the teenage years. It is important to understand that the personal convictions that are forged out together in a family will more likely be built into the teenager's character than those convictions that are pressed upon the adolescent.

My favorite analogy of parenting is that of a parent flying a kite. During the adolescent years, the wise parent is gradually letting out more and more of the string of the kite, giving the teenager more and more freedom. The loving parent understands that at times, the kite may become stuck in a tree, and the parent helps the adolescent to understand how to break free again. And, then, one day, the string is released entirely as the child becomes an emotionally healthy young adult. Corrie Ten Boom put it wisely when she wrote, "I have learned to hold onto everyone loosely."

An important insight to understand in the "letting go" process is this paradox: The more that the parent encourages the adolescent to think for himself, the more the teenager will care about what the parent thinks. I have found this to be true with my own son and daughter over and over again. Conversely, the more controlling the parent becomes, the more difficult the release of an emotionally healthy child will be.

One mother who has adult children writes: *"The first child to leave, whether it is for college, career, or marriage, usually gives the greatest jolt emotionally. The old strings resist being loosened, but God intended our children to be their own persons. And, the greatest favor that we can do is to let them go. The reward of truly releasing our children is that such a parent, without asking for it, gains her adult children's friendship as well as their love. The very special relationship that we now have with our adult children provides us a continued glow which warms our hearts in the home where they no longer live."*

A very wise mother!

Those of us who are Christians especially remember a Father who released his Son. Our Divine Father set His Son free, the Son who came to earth to teach us how to live, and to show us how to love, and to go to the cross sacrificially for us. Because our Loving Father was willing to release His Son, we are redeemed, and we now can be in that tender process of gradually releasing our children in their adolescent years, and offering them to God as spiritually and emotionally healthy young adults.

Chapter 7

A Healthy Parent will understand how to build self-worth into the lives of his or her children.

"Children's antennae are constantly tuned into the way their parents interpret the trials and struggles of life."

Dr. Martin Seligman

I can remember as I anticipated becoming a parent one day, I began to sense in a growing way that I was lacking in my own self-worth. I realized even more that if this was true, then it was going to be very difficult for me as a parent to build self-worth into the lives of my children. Lack of self-worth is something to be dealt with because one consequence of not valuing ourselves is that it will negatively impact our children.

For many months, I drove a long distance from where I lived in the mid-west to St. Paul, Minnesota to meet with a Christian counselor who had been recommended to me because of his expertise in helping people to grow in their sense of self-worth. I came to understand and experience that only as we truly love ourselves are we then free to get out of ourselves, and to really focus on the deepest needs of our children.

John Powell, author of <u>The Christian Vision</u> makes this helpful analogy: imagine suffering from a severe toothache. He suggests that anyone who is living with a toothache finds it to be very difficult to focus on anyone else because the pain is so intense. He then goes on to argue that the agony of a toothache is a lot like a parent who has a low sense of self-worth. He lives with so much pain from the brokenness in his own life that it is difficult for him to say to himself, "Even in the midst of this, I'm going to get out of myself, and really focus on drawing out all the dreams and the deepest needs of my children's lives."

What are the signs of a lack of self-worth in a child? Very often, a child who is needy in this area will put up defenses: "I don't feel very good about myself, so I'll become the class bully. I'll push everyone else around because if I can put my classmates down, it will build me up."

Another way that a child might express his pain is by withdrawing: "I'm just going to live in isolation. I'm going to be very shy. If I relate to other children at all, it will be with much younger children. I feel more secure with them." I can relate to that defense mechanism from my own childhood.

A third example of a child who hasn't developed positive self-worth is one who chooses to conform. If his peer group regularly drinks alcohol, he'll be prone to be involved with it, too. He isn't secure enough to set boundaries, to take a stand, and be able to say, "No, I don't drink!"

The "Class Clown" is frequently someone who lacks self-worth. By creating an environment where others laugh at him, he gets the attention that he craves. One Christian psychologist writes: "By making an enormous joke out of everything, the class clown conceals the low self-worth that churns inside."

Wise parents understand that when self-worth is not present, children will put up one or more of dozens of defenses. We need to be able to know our children well enough that we can articulate, "This is the defense that my child is creating, and this is the strategy that I have to break down that defense, and to build up his self-worth."

How do we help our children overcome those defenses, and learn to value and esteem themselves for a lifetime? I offer four practical strategies.

First, become deeply involved in your child's life. From the time that our children were very young, I began to do a significant amount of research in what is called, "Triangular Communication." Triangular Communication is the process whereby a parent has a passion to be creating all sorts of activities where there is this triangle: there is me as the parent, there is my child, and there is this activity that we are doing *together*. There is strong evidence that every parent needs to work diligently at triangular communication if he is hoping to have an authentic relationship with his or her child.

When a parent is passionate about creating all kinds of triangular activities from the time his child is very young, then out of those activities that are done *together,* the child senses that his parent loves him deeply. The child begins to realize that he has a sense of worth and value because the parent is so fully involved in his life!

For example, from the time that Rachael was little, she loved to ride her bike, and so we would ride bikes *together.* When she was a little older, she liked to do "Step Aerobics," and we went to class *together.* We continued with pursuing her interests through her junior and senior high years that included running, playing basketball, visiting the music store and choosing "CDs," and more.

As parents, we discover a myriad of ways that enable us to create triangular activities. The format of activities will change along with the interests that our children have. We have to be creative enough to make adjustments all the way through the adolescent years. In the process of doing the activities together, communication begins to take place. *Communication* builds the relationship with the child who is experiencing the reality that his parent is deeply involved in his life.

Research confirms that one of the least effective ways to interact with your child is to go to him and ask, "How's it going?" or "How was school today?" Those kinds of questions usually elicit a one word response like "Fine." Our efforts to communicate with our children in that way will be futile, especially as they move toward adolescence. Instead, requests like: "Tell me about your day."

"Why did you choose this library book?" *"I* want to hear about the picture that you made" promote thought on the child's part, and a more meaningful response.

Second, initiate a plan to help your child compensate for an area of weakness with an area of strength. Compensate, as it applies here, means that we parents need to find something that our children can do well to help them counterbalance an area that isn't as developed as it could be when they mature, or that is always going to be a challenge.

For example, a child who doesn't make particularly good grades in our grade worshipping culture can still come to a healthy sense of self-worth. If he has a parent who, with God's help, is committed to finding an activity or characteristic where he is "gifted" and that he enjoys, that will help him compensate for areas where he stumbles or struggles. All of us have those areas.

Years ago, I knew a father who had a great desire to find something that his special needs son could do *well.* He was passionate about finding something that could compensate for the many areas where his boy was not successful. His unconditional love caused him to search relentlessly, and finally, he discovered that his son could throw the shotput. This boy became a conference champion at the shotput, and his self-worth began to grow and to blossom.

One of my favorite authors, Dr. Jay Kesler who was President of "Youth for Christ" for many years, wrote these words: "Every child needs a niche, and it is far more important that we help our children find their own area of expertise than that we try to satisfy our own desires for achievement by getting our children to do what we love doing or always wanted to do when we were children. Children need to wholeheartedly buy into whatever they are doing.

"The best way for parents to encourage this is to be enthusiastic about the things their children are enthusiastic about rather than constantly throwing cold water on their ideas.

"Frankly, this has been one of the more interesting challenges for me as a parent. It is not easy for me to keep my enthusiasm for ideas that I am pretty sure will be short-lived. I have realized, however, that even if I don't believe in the idea, I must believe in my child."

One Christian psychologist and author puts it this way: "A child who doesn't make high grades can still have self-worth in an academically challenging school. He compensates for his lack by excelling in another field. In so doing, he learns to love himself properly by doing well in that realm rather than in the realm of grades where he does so poorly."

Dr. James Dobson writes: "One of the most vital tools for any parent is a process called compensation. It means the individual counterbalances his weaknesses by capitalizing on his strength. It is our job as parents to help our children find their strengths. Perhaps he is gifted in music. Perhaps he can develop his artistic talent, learn to write, or cultivate mechanical skills, or build model airplanes, or raise rabbits for fun and profit. Regardless of what the choice is, the key is to start him down the road early!" Dr. Dobson concludes, "There is nothing more risky than sending a teenager into the storms of adolescence with no skills, no unique knowledge, no means of compensating." Compensation: a truly great strategy for building self-worth!

Third, commit yourself to building into your child a positive vision toward life. Author John Powell argues convincingly in one of his many books that one of the greatest gifts a parent can ever give to his child is a positive perspective of life. And, conversely, research suggests that if you as a parent have a critical spirit, and you have an essentially negative vision toward life, that spirit very likely will be passed on to your son or daughter. If you are a parent, and your spouse, family members, and friends convey to you that you tend to have a critical spirit, that is a matter to commit daily to God in prayer.

In regard to this third strategy, the writings of Dr. Martin Seligman, the pioneer of the positive psychology movement in this country, have been extremely insightful to me. He writes, "Children's antennae are constantly tuned into the way their parents, particularly their mothers, interpret the trials and struggles of life. It is no accident that 'Why' is one of the first and most repeated questions that young children ask. If the parent interprets the trials and struggles of life with a negative and defeatist demeanor, this will have a profound influence on the life of the child."

One son, who had parents who constantly modeled a positive perspective toward life, wrote this love letter to his mom and dad, paraphrasing excerpts from the poems by Elizabeth Barrett Browning and Roy Croft.

"Dear Mom and Dad,

I love you not only for what you are, but for what I am when I'm with you. I love you not only for what you have made of yourself, but for what you are making of me. I love you for putting your hand into my broken heart, and for drawing out into the light all the beautiful belongings that no one else had looked quite far enough to find.

Mom and Dad, I love you because you are helping me to make out of the lumber of my life not a tavern, but a temple."

Like the parents described in this letter, we are to commit ourselves to building into our children a positive perspective toward life.

Fourth, be passionately dedicated to helping your child understand who he is in Christ. A healthy Christian parent will model, has experienced in his heart, and is constantly conveying to his children both verbally and non-verbally:

1. You are extravagantly and unconditionally loved by God.

2. You have been wonderfully formed and created in the very image of God.

3. God loves you so deeply that if you'd been the only person to have ever lived, He would've sent His only son, Jesus Christ to die for you.

4. Through Christ, you can do all things for He comes alongside you to strengthen you!

Ultimately, as we desire to build self-worth in our children's lives, we have a passion to first experience it in our own hearts, and then to pass on to our children how lavishly, relentlessly, and exuberantly they are loved by God. In this humanistic culture, this Biblical strategy more than any other is going to make the ultimate difference in the self-worth that our sons and daughters will have all the days of their lives.

CHAPTER 8

A Healthy Parent will enable his or her child to understand how to develop and maintain good friends.

"Friendship has been the sheltering tree of my life."

Samuel Taylor Coleridge

I was deeply honored to officiate at the wedding of my daughter Rachael. I remember the bridesmaids she chose. Cari and Michelle, two Christian friends from her childhood days, and Jocelyn, a wonderful Mormon friend from high school. There were Kimberly, Carrie, and Peggy, three Christian friends from her time in college. Then, ultimately, standing beside her, the greatest friendship she had developed over her years at Westmont College, her future husband Justin.

I believe that Rachael is more for God today because all of her life, she has been able to choose, build, and maintain good friendships. It is a deeply crucial social need that we as healthy Christian parents must be concerned about for our children.

One of the greatest social needs that every child has is to learn how to choose, build, and maintain good friendships. So much so that one Christian psychologist writes that the three major goals that every Christian parent ought to focus on with his children are these:

First, that my children would love Christ.

Second, that my children would have a healthy sense of self-worth.

Third, that my children would be able to choose and maintain good friends.

Since Chapter 9 of this book is devoted to learning the important process of helping our children to find their own place to stand in relationship with Christ, and in Chapter 7, there are guidelines for helping our children to develop self-worth in their lives, in this chapter, I'll seek to give some practical guidance about helping our children choose and maintain good friends.

Most of what our children will learn about making good friends they will learn from us. They will watch us, and then ask themselves in their own hearts, "What kinds of friends does Mom have? Does Dad have friends who love God? Do they have friends who live their lives with integrity? Do Mom and Dad have friends who are going to tempt them to compromise their values? Do their friends love them unconditionally?"

I'm deeply grateful that my parents created an environment in our home that encouraged the development of enduring friendships. Not only did they choose quality, loving people of integrity for their friends, but, they also nurtured a setting in our home that was inviting to all in the neighborhood. Mom and Dad created an atmosphere in our home which caused me to think "If there's a friend sleepover planned for tonight, I'd rather sleep over at my home than at my friend's because it's always so much fun here."

My father, a kind and compassionate Christian pastor, developed a youth ministry that featured sports, parties, and hayrides along with Bible study and group prayer times. When one of us in the group made a mistake, there was gentle discipline combined with unconditional love.

During my high school years, I forged out friendships with three young men who were all in Dad's youth group with me. These friends, Pedro Garcia, Bill Richardson, and Bob Mazawa have remained close friends with me for over 50 years, and have helped to shape my life in many ways. Looking back, I recognize that my parents created an environment that encouraged me to develop and maintain good friends.

When my children were growing up in our home, I was particularly mindful of three skills that are crucial for building and preserving good friends:

First, conversational: *for example, the ability to articulate in a kind and clear way.*

Second, relational: *for example, the ability to show empathy and compassion.*

Third, emotional self-monitoring: *for example, the ability to resolve conflict in healthy ways.*

Foundational to all three of these skills is the crucial fifth habit in Stephen Covey's classic, best-selling book, <u>The Seven Habits of Highly Effective People</u> which I mention in Chapter 5.

The fifth habit reads, "Seek first to understand, then to be understood." A healthy parent leads the way in consistently modeling this challenging habit in his or her family, so that the child can truly understand the importance of this pivotal skill as it relates to enduring friendships.

In regularly practicing this habit, the parent seeks to empathetically listen to his child, genuinely attempting to understand how the child feels. The parent does not engage in active listening with the goal of framing a response to the words of the child. Rather this reflective listening is motivated solely for the purpose of understanding the child's perspective which often will be far different than the position taken by the parent. Particularly during the adolescent years, no habit served our family as well as this habit. Often Rachael's and Nathan's view of a situation would be in direct contrast to mine. However, *honoring* them by first seeking to authentically understand their viewpoint, vulnerable and open communication often took place.

As I watched my children choose and maintain friendships, I often observed that as they compassionately practiced Covey's fifth habit, their relationships deepened. When conflicts arose, they were generally resolved in an atmosphere of caring and positive problem solving that had been created through their experience with this powerful habit.

When my brother Paul was diagnosed with a rapidly spreading cancer that would take his life at the age of forty-one, both Paul and I relied upon family and friends to help sustain us. I frequently flew from my California home to Denver to be with my brother in the final weeks of his life. Often, I slept overnight in his hospital room with him on a spare bed graciously provided to me. After his death, I flew to Denver to support his wife and two young sons, and to help plan the memorial service which I would lead. During those days, I was in frequent contact with three friends who lived in California. When they called one day, I asked how things were going back home. To my complete surprise, they said, "Actually, Ron, we're not calling from California. We're calling from a motel in Denver. We flew in last night just to be here to support you in any way that we can in the days ahead." I wept as I experienced the deep love of these friends for me and my family in a time of devastating loss. I know that this expression of friendship had a significant impact upon my children.

I deeply believe that if we yearn for our children to demonstrate the attribute of being able to develop and maintain good friends, we must first model that quality in our own lives. Hopefully, our children see the quality of friendships that we are building, and begin to develop those same relationships in their own lives. When they graduate from our homes, and move into adulthood, we will have been a link in God's chain to better enable them to be in love with Christ, to have a healthy, Christ-centered sense of self-worth, and to be able to build and maintain Godly friendships. If we have done that, we will sense that one day we shall hear from our Savior, "Well done, thou good and faithful servant."

CHAPTER 9

A Healthy Parent will demonstrate by his or her life that Jesus Christ is the Lord of his or her heart.

"Nothing happens through us that isn't happening to us."

Dr. Ron Lee Davis

Futurologists and sociologists John Naisbitt, Daniel Bell, Alvin Toffler, Nathan Glazer, and Manual Castells have provided helpful insights as we seek to understand the rapidly changing culture in which our families live today. In general terms, they help us to understand that there have been three primary eras, three periods of history that we have experienced in American culture. It is of crucial importance for us to understand the implications of these three eras for us as individuals and for our children.

The first era was **agricultural.** It was the time of the little house on the prairie. It was the period in history when the husband and wife, the parent and child worked side by side in the field or in the kitchen, day after day, *together.* The pioneer was seeking to forge out his crops, his home, and his family which was almost always an extended one with grandparents, aunts, uncles, and cousins living very nearby, or often in the same home.

The next era was **industrial**. We migrated from the country to the city. We were no longer developing our own farms and crops by hand. Now we were working in factories with machinery. The extended family was not always nearby. In fact, it was sometimes extended out into different cities far away. The family was smaller: the husband, wife, two to four or more children who became known as the "nuclear family."

The third era in cultural history was referred to as the **information** era. This era has been fast-paced, and includes amazing technology. It has had tremendous implications, and often negative impact upon the family. The late futurologist Alvin Toffler stated, "A powerful wave is surging across much of the world today creating a new and often bizarre environment in which to raise children. In this bewildering context, value systems splinter and crash while the lifeboats of family and church are hurled madly about. The third era makes a quantum leap from what we have known in the familiar waters of yesterday to the uncharted course of tomorrow."

Just as there were three eras for American culture, we discover in scripture that there were three eras for the children of Israel centuries ago. The first for the Israelites was **slavery in Egypt**. For five hundred years, there was bondage. But, at least there was security there, three meager meals a day, and a hut to sleep in at night with your family.

Then, there emerged an eighty year old leader named Moses who led the people out of Egypt. He led an exodus into the second era, which was marked by **wandering in the wilderness**. The Israelites were no longer living in the culture of Egypt, but were led by a cloud during the day, and by a pillar of fire by night.

After forty years, the Israelites prepared to move into their third era, **the Promised Land**. As the children of Israel were about to enter this new land, Moses gathered the people together, and in Deuteronomy 6, he says, in essence, these words: As you are about ready to go into Canaan, the land of milk & honey, you are also going into a place that is spiritually decadent. I want to share with you some guidelines for families who are moving into this new period.

Four principles emerge from these verses for families in the third era in Canaan and for families in the midst of contemporary culture.

1. **A love for God is to permeate the parent**. Deuteronomy 6:5 says, "*You shall love the Lord your God with all your heart, and with all your soul, and with all your strength.*" In the Hebrew text, whenever there is a repetition of one word, three times in a sentence, as in the word "all" in this verse, it conveys the idea of "to permeate." A love for God is to *permeate* from my life to my children. It is impossible for me to transfer to my child that which I do not personally embrace.

For example: it's impossible for me to transfer the importance of compassion to my child if I do not extend compassion to him. It is impossible for me to convey to my child that he does not need to rely on drugs if I have a growing reliance upon alcohol in my own life.

The same is true for our love for God. It is impossible for me to convey a love for God to my child a love for God does not permeate my life. Nothing happens through me that isn't happening to me.

Accordingly, the greatest concern for us as Christian parents is that we are growing spiritually. The operative word in this principle is "permeate." Permeate literally means, "to pass through the pores of something. A Christian parent understands that his love for God must pass through the pores of his life in order for his children to be able to see His love daily. In this regard, a helpful prayer that I have offered every morning for many years is, "May my life be a sweet aroma of the love and compassion of Christ to all I touch today."

2. **Consistently teaching the truths of scripture is essential.** In Deuteronomy 6:7, Moses tells us that we are to diligently teach our children God's truth as we talk with them. The Hebrew word that is used here is "talk," as it carries with it the idea of sharing in a conversational style, much as we would converse about anything else. It is

to be the natural communication of truth from one generation to the next. If Christianity is going to be authentic, our faith needs to be communicated to our children so that they experience it in a daily lifestyle.

Moses says that the methodology to be used in the transfer of faith from one generation to another is to be non-structured. He says that you shall talk of God when you sit down, walk, lie down, and rise up. You kneel down beside your daughter's bed, and she's got a problem. The most natural thing in the world is to talk about how God can help with it. It's Monday morning, and your son is feeling anxious about going to school. You get down to his level, put your hand on his shoulder, and say a simple, brief prayer that assures him that God is going to help him today. We parents are set free from having to segment Christianity. It no longer just fits on a certain day of the week, or only in activities like Sunday School and church.

There is a world of difference between doing religious things, and being authentically Christian. We who are Christian parents are constantly doing self-evaluation in our hearts asking, "Am I just playing religious games, or am I being authentically, genuinely Christian with my children?"

3. **Have a tender heart filled with gratitude for God's provision.** In Deuteronomy 6:10-12, Moses says essentially: As you're about to enter a spiritually decadent land, take heed lest you forget the Lord because He's the one who brought you out of bondage. He says the very same thing to us today. In the midst of the self-absorbed culture that surrounds us, every Christian parent ought to seek to model daily Isaiah 26:12 for his children. It's really a prayer, and reads, "Lord, all that we have accomplished, You have done for us." Maybe we've worked hard for thirty or forty years to obtain what we have, and our children have seen that, but the demeanor of the Christian parent in front of his family should be an attitude that softly models this verse: *Loving God, your blessings are beyond our deserving. It's all been your grace. We give the glory to You. Thank You for your loving kindness to our family.*

I cannot begin to tell you the number of times that I would slip by my Dad's den, or by Mom's and Dad's bedroom, and the door would be open just a crack, that I would see Dad kneeling in prayer, early in the morning, midday, or late at night. He was modeling for me, as he prayed, "Loving God, I yearn to have a humble heart filled with gratitude, and I want to pass that spirit on to my boys."

4. **Frequently recall God's faithfulness in times past with your children, that they might trust in the Lord for all of their tomorrows.** In Deuteronomy 6:20, Moses conveys the idea that in the future, our child may come to us and want to know about how things used to be. Moses is very clear, and he says, "Parents, what you're to tell your child is this, 'We used to be in bondage, but God did some miraculous things, and He set us free. Let me tell you the stories of God's faithfulness in past times so that you can trust God for all of your days.'"

My mom was unquestionably the single most influential person in my life. Before her death, I talked with her every day. She lived with severe chronic pain, and was totally unable to walk. She had lost her only other child, and her husband many years before. Yet, when we would talk, her spirit constantly communicated to me, "God's been faithful, Ron. He's been faithful to the Davis family. He's always been faithful, and He will be faithful in what I'm facing now."

My mother loved the old hymn "Great is Thy Faithfulness," especially this verse:

"Great is thy faithfulness, O God, my Father.
There is no shadow of turning with Thee.
Thou changest not, thy compassions, they
fail not.
As thou hast been, thou forever wilt be."

It is of such comfort to a child to have a parent who, even in the midst of severe pain and very difficult circumstances, still communicates God's incredible faithfulness yesterday, today, and forever.

These four principles are great truths that we seek to transfer to our children. They will serve them well in their hours of greatest need, when we are no longer with them, perhaps no longer on this earth so that we might know that we have helped to build the very character of God into our children's lives.

"Children are a gift from God;
they are His reward."

Psalms 127:3

CHAPTER 10

A Healthy Parent is committed to process.

"Parenting is a lifelong process of modeling unconditional love. In every family there will be seasons of joy and seasons of sorrow. There will be seasons of obedience and seasons of rebellion. The Christian mother and father must set the pace in modeling the reality that parenting is a lifelong process lived out together with our children in love."

Dr. Ron Lee Davis

It was Christmas time, many years ago. A little boy named Moss Hart and his father decided that they would travel by subway to downtown New York City to shop at a large discount department store. Their objective was to find one Christmas present for little Moss. His father was a poor man. He worked hard, but he toiled in a factory where the weekly wages he received were very small.

Moss knew exactly what he wanted for Christmas. He wanted either a miniature chemistry set or a beginner's printing press. His loving father had much less expensive gifts in mind. Up and down the aisles of the huge department they walked. After a long time had passed, Moss would find a toy that he liked. His father would then ask the store salesman, "How much would this toy cost?" Upon hearing the price, the father would gently shake his head and quietly respond, "I don't think this is what we had in mind."

Then, as the father and son walked a bit further along in the store, the father would find a less expensive toy, and show it to his boy. As much as Moss tried to pretend that he liked the toy, he really didn't want it. His discerning father could recognize his son's disappointment; he would place the toy back silently. This process continued until Moss and his father reached the very last aisle, and still, there was no Christmas present. The father and son left the store empty-handed.

Years later, Moss Hart would reflect upon this experience: "I heard my father jingle some coins in his pocket, and I knew it all in a flash. Dad had pulled together about seventy-five cents to buy me a Christmas present, but he had not dared say so in case there was nothing to be had for so small a sum. As I looked at him, I saw a look of despair and disappointment in his eyes that brought me closer to him than I had ever been before in my life. I wanted to throw my arms around him and say, 'It doesn't matter, Daddy. It doesn't matter. I understand. Just being with you is better than any old printing press. I love you, Daddy. I love you.'

"But, instead, we just stood there shivering beside each other for a moment, and then we started silently back home. I didn't even take his hand on the way home, nor did he take mine.

We were not on that basis. Nor did I ever tell him how close I felt to him on that night, that for a little while, the concrete wall between father and son crumbled away, and I knew that we were just two lonely people struggling to reach each other."

What is it about those of us who are fathers? Call it pride, cultural training, macho reserve: many fathers even against the true yearning of their hearts, create an invisible wall that causes a separation between themselves and their families. As Moss Hart put it, "two lonely people struggling to reach each other, but we were not on that basis." Yet, I would affirm from Scripture that we human beings were *made* to be on that basis, to be in loving, vulnerable, expressive, and transparent, relationships with one another.

Gary Crosby, eldest son of the Bing Crosby family, understood the moat-like distance that can separate a father from his family. Gary had a father who attained a great deal of success in the world's eyes as a singer and actor. Yet, he writes these words about his dad: "My father was an excellent communicator professionally, but found himself totally unable to express love for his own children. He could not express joy and affirmation in any words that we could even understand. Because of his inability to communicate love, our entire family suffered terribly."

As we come to the conclusion of the book, I want to reflect on the importance of understanding parenting as a lifelong process of modeling unconditional love. One aspect of this process is how the parent leads the way in helping his or her children to always take the long view. He or she understands that in every family, if we strip away all of the false veneers, there will be seasons of joy and seasons of sorrow. There will be peaks and valleys. There will be seasons of obedience, and of rebellion. But, we take the long view because we understand that parenting is a *process* in our lives together with our children.

Put another way, healthy parents never count the score at halftime. Some of you may be counting the score with one of your children. You may have a child who is far away from God, and may be far away from you as a parent, as well. But, it's only halftime; the game isn't over yet.

We are in this with God through all eternity. Often seasons of rebellion and doubt lead a child to a deeper faith than he or she has ever known before. Healthy parents are committed to process, but here's the catch: process takes tremendous sacrifice. It might be observed in a dad sitting up with his elementary age daughter because she can't sleep. She's afraid of someone at school who has been known to bully other children. He sacrifices as he stays with her, and tries to ease her fears.

Sacrifice can take the form of an ongoing experience such as a mother waiting year after year for one of her children to come back to Christ. Sometimes it's the sacrifice of watching an adolescent with tremendous potential throwing away that gift because of a compulsive addictive behavior that has now entered his or her life. As Christian parents, we sacrifice, we don't quit, we press on.

Sacrifice is an attribute that isn't popular in American culture. Sociological research conducted over the past generation clearly indicates that many parents are unwilling to sacrifice their own self-fulfillment in order to meet the needs of their children. As Christian parents we must constantly be on guard lest we allow this mindset to infiltrate our relationships with our children.

Indeed, A.W. Tozer states one of the greatest truths of the Christian life when he writes these words: "Every Christian must learn to endure one of two pains: either the pain of double-mindedness or the pain of the crucified self." Every Christian parent is going to have to live from here on out, for the rest of his or her life, experiencing one of those pains. In double-mindedness, we live with one foot with our families, and the other in the world. With the crucified self, we choose to say, "For the rest of my life, I am willing to sacrifice for the cause of these children and the legacy that I can leave as they grow up with God." This is what the apostle Paul implied in Galations 2:20 when he wrote, "*I am crucified with Christ, nevertheless I live, yet not I, but Christ who lives in me.*"

All of the research suggests that in terms of the impact that a parent has on his child, 7% comes from his words, 15% comes from shared experiences (vacations, baseball games, etc.), and 78% from modeling. Our children watch us as Christian parents. They observe, and they contemplate and conclude that we are going to be with them through the long haul. We are going to be there because we are committed to process. We refuse to count the score at halftime.

Years ago, I was speaking at a "Youth for Christ" gathering, and Tony Campolo, a respected Christian author and seminary professor was also addressing the conference. He shared this story. He said that he and his wife, Peggy were often invited to university gatherings, cocktail parties, and social mixers. They would mingle with other professional and career oriented men and women. Often, Mrs. Campolo would be asked, "What do you do?" Her usual timid and humble reply was, "Me? Oh, I'm just a mother."

One night after another social gathering, she went home a bit discouraged that she didn't have a professional career to share at those functions. So, late at night, she prayerfully wrote down what she sensed her "job description" was as a Christian mother.

At the next social event, a professional woman asked, "And, what do you do?" Mrs. Campolo replied, "With the help of God, I am socializing three children into the dominant values of the Christian faith so that they might be agents for change, enabling the kingdom of God to triumph victoriously over the dying kingdoms of this world.

Then, she asked the woman, "And, what do you do?" The woman replied, "Oh, I'm just a doctor."

It is a high and holy calling that God in His grace has given to those of us who are parents. When we intentionally choose to invest our lives in our children, we embark upon the most exciting undertaking in life. As we allow all the ten traits to invade our hearts, and involve ourselves with our children in unseen places and quiet moments, our ministry is nearly invisible. Yet, with time, this commitment of our loving God gives us His wisdom and grace as we continue to embark on this grand adventure.

TEN TRAITS OF A HEALTHY PARENT

~~ Dr. Ron Lee Davis

1. A Healthy Parent will demonstrate unconditional love to his or her children, both verbally and nonverbally.

2. A Healthy Parent will seek to value the personhood of each child.

3. A Healthy Parent will take the time to get to know his or her child according to his or her own uniqueness.

4. A Healthy Parent will seek to discern unhealthy intergenerational patterns, and break the cycle of those patterns.

5. A Healthy Parent models a commitment that when problems arise, they are openly confronted and talked through using positive communication skills.

6. A Healthy Parent will understand from the time his or her children are

very young that there are four major struggles every child will face in adolescence.

7. A Healthy Parent will understand how to build self-worth into the lives of his or her children.

8. A Healthy Parent will enable his or her child to understand how to build and maintain good friends.

9. A Healthy Parent will demonstrate by his or her life that Jesus Christ is the Lord of his heart.

10. A Healthy Parent is committed to process.

~ ~ ~

"Clothe yourselves with compassion, kindness, humility, gentleness, and patience. And, above all these virtues, put on love."

Colossians 3:12, 14

STUDY GUIDE

The following study guide will be helpful for your practical application of the principles developed in this book. It can be used either for your own personal study, or in a discussion group setting.

Chapter 1

<u>Trait #1</u> A Healthy Parent will demonstrate unconditional love to his or her children, both verbally and nonverbally.

1. A growing number of Christian psychologists have suggested there are four primary ways we demonstrate unconditional love to a child:

    a. focused attention
    b. eye contact
    c. physical contact
    d. consistent verbal reassurance

As you think back over the past thirty days, which of these four ways has been the most difficult for you to model to your children? Why? What specific action can you take to improve in this area of responsibility to your children?

2. Research developed by Dr. Ross Campbell suggests that men rarely show physical affection to their children. Was this true in your family of origin? As a father or mother, do you demonstrate consistent physical affection to your children? Why, or why not?

3. While the term "unconditional love" has gained broad acceptance in our society, in reality, it is often not understood or practiced within our homes. When one of your children intentionally disobeys you, mistreats a sibling, or performs poorly on a school assignment due to a lack of preparation, how do you as a parent continue to demonstrate your unconditional love to him or her?

Chapter 2

<u>Trait #2</u> A Healthy Parent will seek to value the personhood of each child.

1. We value the personhood of each child in the following five ways:

    a. by respecting our children's opinions
    b. by respecting each child's privacy
    c. by trusting our children
    d. by taking the time to get to know each child by the longhand of personhood
    e. by believing in each child's dreams

Which of these five strategies for valuing the personhood of our children needs the most work in your life as a parent? What specific action could you take to improve in that strategy?

2. Over the past four decades, we have been hearing and reading about a term called "toxic shame." One great way to shame your child is to constantly distrust him, to communicate in all sorts of ways that as your child, he or she is in no way trustworthy.

Do you agree with this statement? How can you avoid "toxic shaming" with your children when trust is broken, when a child is deceptive?

3. Expectation tends to foretell performance. Do you believe that you intentionally communicate to your children that you believe in them and know that they are going to be someone great for God? Why, or why not?

4. Fred Rogers writes, "Children have very deep feelings just the way parents do, and are striving to understand these feelings and to better respond to them is what I feel is the most important task in our world." As a parent, how do you intentionally seek to discover the deepest feelings of your children?

5. A paraphrase of Proverbs 20:5 could read: A dream in the heart of a child is like deep water, but the understanding parent draws it out. How do you as a parent seek "to draw out the dreams" of your children? How do you ensure that you are encouraging your children's dreams, rather than what you might want them to pursue?

Chapter 3

<u>Trait #3</u> A Healthy Parent will take the time to get to know his or her child according to his or her own uniqueness.

1. My paraphrase of Proverbs 22:6 reads: Modify the training of each of your children based upon their distinctive, God-given temperaments and unique characteristics, and then, when each child matures, he will not retreat from the guidance that you have given him.

As a parent, do you think that you take the individual temperaments of your children into consideration as you seek to guide them? Give an example.

2. If you have more than one child, do you think that the birth order of each child fits the general characteristics of birth order research as described by Dr. Kevin Leman?

3. Gretchen Rubin's research indicates that there are four primary styles that children have as they relate to expectations placed upon them by parents and teachers:

a. Upholders
b. Questioners

    c. Obligers

    d. Rebels

Can you describe which primary style portrays each of your children? How does that style affect the way in which you relate to each of your children?

4.   Gordon Cosby writes, "One of the foremost responsibilities of parents is to enjoy their children." What are specific ways that you create fun-filled times with your children?

5.   What is one specific way that you could be more sensitive to each of your children as you train, support, and discipline them according to their own uniqueness? Proverbs 22:6

Chapter 4

<u>Trait #4</u> A Healthy Parent will seek to discern unhealthy intergenerational patterns, and to break the cycle of those patterns.

1. In Exodus 34:7 we read, "The sins of the parents shall be visited upon the children and upon the grandchildren, and onto the third and fourth generations." Family systems psychologists have demonstrated that a character flaw or addictive, compulsive behavior in a parent is often also observed in that parents' children. Can you think of a character flaw or addiction that marked one of your parents that you also battled in your own life? Do you see a character flaw or addiction in your own life now emerging in one of your children? What specific steps have you taken to break the cycle of intergenerational character flaws?

2. Three specific commitments that we can make as we seek to counteract intergenerational character flaws:

   a. Devote yourself to experiencing a vital daily walk with God.
   b. Consistently ask God to give you wisdom and discernment as you study and observe

your children and their potential character flaws.

c. Understand that generally an unchecked character flaw will escalate, not diminish, and must therefore be lovingly confronted.

Which of these three commitments needs the most work in your own life as a parent today?

3. "What the very young want, and urgently need first, is not education or socialization, but rather the affection and unhurried attention of their parents." Given the multitude of distractions available to us in contemporary culture, how well do you sense that you are honoring the challenge of this quotation?

Chapter 5

<u>Trait #5</u> A Healthy Parent models a commitment that when problems arise, they are openly confronted and talked through using positive communication skills.

1. Author John Powell developed five levels of communication:

   a. Cliches
   b. Facts and Reports
   c. Opinions and Convictions
   d. Feelings
   e. Maximum truth shared with maximum love.

Powell shares research indicating that most families rarely move beyond levels one, two, and three. How frequently do you and your children share deeply with one another in communication levels four and five?

2. In his book <u>The 7 Habits of Highly Effective People</u>, Stephen Covey shares that the fifth habit, "First seek to understand, then to be understood," is the most difficult of the seven habits to apply to family life. How effective are you in applying this habit when conflict arises with one of your children?

3. Five guidelines when loving confrontation is required with one of your children are:

    a. Be gentle, but firm.
    b. Be certain that you fully understand the situation.
    c. Verbally affirm your love for your child regularly, and throughout the conversation.
    d. Be specific.
    e. Always remember to look past the irritation to the need.

Thinking back on a recent confrontation with one of your children, how would you evaluate yourself on following these five guidelines?

4. The purpose of loving confrontation is to heal, not to cripple. It is to help, not to hurt. It is to restore, not to shame. As a parent, how specifically are you able to put this scriptural principle into practice? Can you give an example of when you were able to follow it?

Chapter 6

<u>Trait #6</u> A Healthy Parent will understand from the time that his or her children are very young, that there are four major struggles that every child will face in adolescence.

1. Years ago, Edith Schaeffer wrote, "My role as a parent is to be a curator in a museum of memories." How intentionally do you create activities with your children that are helping to build wonderful memories in their hearts of growing up in a Christian home?

2. A healthy teenager will wrestle with these four adolescent struggles (identity, responsibility, authority, and conformity), and the responsibility of the parent is to help his or her child work through these transitions. How well do you believe that your parents guided you through the adolescent years? What character qualities do you believe that you will most need to model as your children transition through the teenage years into adulthood?

3. A lifelong study researched by Dr. Nicholas Stinnett caused him and his colleagues to conclude that there are six essential qualities that distinguish strong families.

a. They are deeply committed to one another within the family unit.
b. They spend time together.
c. They learn to intentionally express appreciation for one another.
d. They share a deep spiritual commitment.
e. They have the skills to solve problems together when difficulties arise.
f. They have developed excellent communication skills.

Take a moment to reflect on these six qualities, and ask yourself: As a parent, how well do I model these qualities? Which of the qualities needs the most improvement in my own life?

Chapter 7

<u>Trait #7</u> A Healthy Parent will understand how to build self-worth into the lives of his or her child.

1. Research indicates that when a child is lacking in self-worth, he or she will tend to put up defenses such as playing primarily with younger children, becoming the class bully, easily conforming to peer pressure, etc. As a child, did you struggle with self-worth? Did you tend to put up defenses? Do you see that pattern in one of your children? If so, how are you responding to your child's defenses?

2. As a parent, have you created experiences of "triangular communication" with your children? If so, can you give specific examples? Have you found that these experiences create a deeper bond with your children, and enhance their self-worth?

3. Dr. James Dobson writes, "One of the most vital tools for any parent is a process called 'compensation.' It means that the individual counter balances his weaknesses by capitalizing on his strengths. It is our job as parents to help our children find their strengths. Perhaps he is gifted in music.

Perhaps he can develop his artistic talent, learn to write, or cultivate mechanical skills, or build model airplanes, or raise rabbits for fun and profit. Regardless of what the choices are, the key is to start them down the road early. There is nothing more risky than sending a teenager into the storms of adolescence with no skills, no unique knowledge, no means of compensating."

As a parent, have you initiated opportunities for your children to discover an interest or hobby where they can excel and grow in confidence?

4. Dr. Martin Seligman states, "Children's antennae are constantly tuned into the way that their parents, particularly their mothers, interpret the trials and struggles of life. It is no accident that 'Why?' is one of the most repeated questions that young children ask. If the parent interprets the trials and struggles of life with a negative and defeatist demeanor, this will have a profound influence on the life of the child."

As a parent, do you believe that you are able to interpret struggles that your children face in such a way that they can see the positive side of setbacks and difficult challenges? Can you give a recent example?

5. Do you believe that you intentionally and consistently help your children discover who they are in Christ, and how lovingly God views them?

Chapter 8

<u>Trait #8</u> A Healthy Parent will enable his or her child to understand how to develop and maintain good friends.

1. One essential way that we can enable our children to make good choices about their friends is to model for them the quality of deep friendships that we enjoy as adults with other men and women of integrity and compassion. How effectively are you currently modeling this reality for your children?

2. Three skills that we need to build into our children as they develop friendships with their peers are:

    a. Conversational skills
    b. Relational skills
    c. Emotional self-monitoring

How would you evaluate yourself in building these three skills into the lives of your children?

3. One crucial skill to develop in our own lives and to model for our children is active listening. The parent must seek to listen to his child genuinely attempting to understand how the child feels. The parent does not engage in active listening with the

goal of framing a response to the words of the child.

Rather this active listening is motivated solely for the purpose of understanding the child's perspective which often will be far different than the position taken by the parent.

How effective are you at active listening with your children? Do you sense your children are gradually developing active listening skills with you and with their peers?

Chapter 9

<u>Trait #9</u> A Healthy Parent will demonstrate by his or her life that Jesus Christ is the Lord of his or her life.

1. A love for God must permeate the parent. It is impossible for me to transfer to my child that which I do not personally embrace. Nothing happens through me that isn't happening to me."

Would those who know you best sense that a love for God permeates your life? Do you sense a growing, deeper walk with God in your life?

2. The transfer of faith from one generation to another is to be non-structured. For example, you kneel down beside your daughter's bed, and she's got a problem. The most natural thing in the world is to talk about how God can help with it.

Does this type of non-structured, natural communication of faith seem comfortable to you? Do you feel awkward talking openly about God's love and leading in your home? Why, or why not?

3. Our challenge is to model both gratitude for God's provision and the Recollection of God's faithfulness to our family with our children. Thinking back over the past thirty

days, do you believe you have been intentionally reminding your children of both the gratitude that you have for God's grace and for His faithfulness?

Chapter 10

<u>Trait #10</u> A Healthy Parent is committed to process.

1. Parenting must be viewed as a lifelong process of modeling unconditional love. One aspect of this process is how the parent leads the way in helping his or her children to always take the long view. He or she understands that in every family, if we strip away all of the false veneers, there will be seasons of joy and seasons of sorrow. There will be peaks and valleys. There will be seasons of obedience, and seasons of rebellion. But, we take the long view because we understand that parenting is a process in our lives together with our children. Put another way, healthy parents never count the score at halftime.

When struggles arise with one or more of your children, is it difficult for you to take the long view and recognize that God will honor your perseverance in His timing? What helps you to get through the challenging seasons of parenting?

2. Ron quotes twentieth century pastor and author A.W. Tozer, "Every Christian must learn to endure one of two pains: either the pain of double-mindedness or the pain of

the crucified self." As a parent, do you relate to these words? Do you find it difficult at times to sacrificially give your children the attention and guidance that they need, and in so doing surrender other activities that you enjoy? What strengthens you in this challenge?

3. Ron refers to research that suggests that in terms of the impact that a parent has on his children, 7% comes from his or her words, 15% from shared experiences, and 78% from modeling. In what specific ways could you model a more authentic Christian lifestyle to your children?

4. Review the Ten Traits of a Healthy Parent outlined in this book. Which of the traits do you feel most encouraged about as a Christian parent? Which of the traits needs the most attention and focus in your life today? How specifically could you further build this trait into your life as a parent?

"I'm deeply grateful that my parents created an environment in our home that encouraged the development of enduring friendships. Not only did they choose quality, loving people of integrity for their friends, but they also nurtured a setting in our home that was inviting to all in the neighborhood."

Dr. Ron Lee Davis

ACKNOWLEDGMENTS

Robert Browning, in Pauline (1833) wrote to his friend Shelley, "Live forever, and be to all what you have been to me." I so deeply relate to the sentiment of these words, as so many have loved me, and guided me to a better understanding of the message of this book.

I must first acknowledge my deep gratitude for my parents. Many of the principles outlined in this book were first modeled to me by my mother and father. As my father passed away many years ago, my mom lived for thirty-seven years as a widow, and made countless sacrifices out of her unconditional love for me.

Every word of Washington Irving's tribute to his mother rings true for me. "A mother is the truest friend we have, when trials heavy fall upon us; when adversity takes the place of prosperity; when friends desert us; when trouble thickens around us, still will she cling to us, and endeavor by her kind precepts to dissipate the clouds of darkness, and cause peace to return to our hearts."

My friend, Joanne Bouslough has tirelessly edited, developed, and refined this book. Her efforts are obvious on every page. There would have been no book without her.

Much of the material in this book was first presented at Canyon Creek Presbyterian Church in San Ramon, California, and I am indebted to the wise input of many of the members of that loving congregation. Particularly, the ongoing counsel of my longtime friend, Dave Barry has proved invaluable. Dave is a wonderful Christian father who has shaped my understanding of parenting in many ways.

Next to my own father, the man who shaped many of the truths reflected in the pages of this book were shared with me by Ray Stedman, pastor for forty years of the Peninsula Bible Church in Palo Alto, California. I will always be deeply grateful to Ray and his wise mentoring.

My longtime friend, Stacy Madden has made significant improvements to the content of this book, as well as provided graphic design for the book jacket. Her deep Christian faith inspires me to seek to follow Christ more faithfully.

Special thanks to Ann Golay, a gifted Christian educational psychologist whose wise insights guided me in the development of each chapter of our book.

Marriage and Family Therapist Sarah Douglas has provided outstanding guidance, support, and wisdom in my own journey toward discovering greater wholeness and maturity as a father and grandfather.

The writings of the following authors have been extremely helpful to me in better understanding parenting, family systems research, cultural trends, and/or the nature of unconditional love: Henri Nouwen, Kevin Leman, David Elkind, Jay Kesler, Burton White, Charles Swindoll, J. Keith Miller, Nicholas Stinnett, Tim Kimmel, John Powell, Martin Seligman, John Naisbitt, Bruce Larson, Meg Meeker, Steven Covey, Elizabeth Elliott, Gordon Cosby, Robert Bella, Ross Campbell, Gretchen Rubin, Albert Schweitzer, John Robbins, Tedd Tripp, James Dobson, Alvin Toffler, and Edith Schaeffer.

Finally, and most importantly, my two children, Rachael and Nathan have constantly helped me to understand what it means to be a spiritually and emotionally healthy parent. Their patience, unconditional love, friendship, and compassion have motivated me to continue in this lifelong process of seeking to become a more effective parent. Being a father to Rachael and Nathan has brought me such joy and meaning. The imprint of their lives is found throughout this book.

ABOUT THE AUTHOR

Dr. Ron Lee Davis is the author of several best-selling Christian books.

He has addressed conferences on parenting oriented themes in Asia, Europe, Africa, and throughout the U.S.

Dr. Davis has served as the Bible teacher for both the Minnesota Vikings and the Oakland Athletics. He received his doctoral degree from Bethel University after concluding his under graduate studies at the University of London.

Ron is a father and grandfather who lives in Santa Barbara, California, where he enjoys playing with his four grandchildren, jogging on the beach, and writing a column that has been read widely by thousands in the U. S. and many other countries.

"While the term 'unconditional love' has gained broad acceptance in our society, in reality, it is often not understood nor is it practiced within our homes." -- Dr. Ron Lee Davis

<> <> <> <> <> <> <> <> <> <> <> <> <> <> <>

Over the past twenty-five years, Dr. Davis has presented his series, "Ten Traits of a Healthy Parent" at various churches, conferences, retreats, and adult education classes. This book is the end result of many years of writing, teaching, and refining the material from Ron's series. Foundational to an understanding of the Ten Traits is the first trait: A Healthy Parent will demonstrate unconditional love to his or her children, both verbally and nonverbally.

37083248R00087

Made in the USA
Columbia, SC
02 December 2018